BRIGHT

THE IMMORALIST AND OTHER WORKS BY ANDRÉ GIDE

Intelligent Education

INFLUENCE PUBLISHERS

Nashville, Tennessee

BRIGHT NOTES: The Immoralist and Other Works
www.BrightNotes.com

No part of this publication may be used or reproduced in any manner whatsoever without written permission, except in the case of brief quotations in critical articles and reviews. For permissions, contact Influence Publishers http://www.influencepublishers.com.

ISBN: 978-1-645420-20-0 (Paperback)
ISBN: 978-1-645420-21-7 (eBook)

Published in accordance with the U.S. Copyright Office Orphan Works and Mass Digitization report of the register of copyrights, June 2015.

Originally published by Monarch Press.
Armand Schwerner, 1966
2020 Edition published by Influence Publishers.

Interior design by Lapiz Digital Services. Cover Design by Thinkpen Designs.

Printed in the United States of America.

Library of Congress Cataloging-in-Publication Data forthcoming.
Names: Intelligent Education
Title: BRIGHT NOTES: The Immoralist and Other Works
Subject: STU004000 STUDY AIDS / Book Notes

CONTENTS

ANDRÉ GIDE

. . . .

BEGINNINGS

André Gide, born in Paris in 1869 - he died in 1951 - is one of the most important figures in the literary history of France in the twentieth century. His significance derives not only from his work or his achievements as a stylist but also from his symbolic position as a man of letters over a long life-span. He was the friend or respected antagonist of most of the important French writers during the six decades of his productive and controversial career.

Gide's father died when the boy was eleven years old. Paul Gide was known as an extremely intelligent man, a professor in the faculty of law at the University of Paris. The father's family had a long Protestant tradition in mainly Catholic France, a fact of great philosophical and psychological importance for André Gide, whose mother had also been brought up as a Protestant - although her family had counted among its members a few Roman Catholics. The atmosphere in the home was acutely puritan and moralistic, and left on the novelist an imprint whose profound markings - for all of his ideational struggles -

he never erased. Martin Turnell, a most perceptive Gide critic and biographer, has discussed Gide's own assessment of his maternal and paternal inheritances. In his *Journals* Gide has discussed these inheritances in terms of opposites which make for dramatic juxtapositions, but which may also demonstrate the love of symmetry so typical of the French literary mind. Paul Gide's family had lived in Uzès, a town in southern France not far from the Mediterranean; Juliette Gide came from Normandy. But although Albert Guerard, another important critic and biographer of Gide, quotes an opinion citing the intellectuality of Uzès and the sensuousness of Normandy, he agrees with Turnell that no simple oppositions can be constructed between the two regions - whose attributes a visitor might in fact confuse with each other. The observation points up Gide's turning toward classicism and symmetry, the great concern for clarity of expression which has made his style the object of much study and admiration. As we shall see, however, another major aspect of the novelist's character, rebellious and iconoclastic, contended with the first; the conflict gave rise to the kinds of conflicts which would produce the works under discussion in this Study Guide.

André, whose childhood was sickly, was brought up in an atmosphere markedly defined by the presence of women in the household and in important positions. The father's early death served to emphasize the repressive presence of austerity. Besides Gide's mother, there was Anna Shackleton, originally Juliette Gide's governess, the daughter of a Scotch engineer settled in France, a spinster. Two important teachers were women; there was an aunt, Claire, intensely middle-class, a woman of probity. Mme. Gide had decided early to protect her son from the contamination of unhealthy influences. She saw to it that he had piano lessons, but - Guerard remarks - made sure that he did not play Chopin, a composer she regarded as a bad influence. There was money in the family; indeed Gide never had to worry about that; but she made her son account closely for his allowance even after the inception of his writing career.

Another woman, however, played a highly important part in Gide's life, early and late: Madeleine Rondeaux. Although Gide did experience a rather lonely, isolated childhood, and although his friendships were limited largely to members of the family, he did have friends. Madeleine was Gide's cousin. One night, when Gide was a boy of thirteen - he was visiting his uncle Émile, Madeleine's father - he came upon his already beloved Madeleine kneeling by her bed, weeping bitter tears: the young girl had just discovered her mother's adulterous activities, which would eventually split up the family. Gide wrote much later about this incident, which he described as the discovery of a mystic orientation of his life. He was deeply moved by her misery and decided that he would devote his entire life to an attempt to cure her of her unhappiness. From that time on the two children shared all holidays, read the same books, became intensely concerned with similar matters. In addition little Madeleine was immensely religious, and through her Gide read the Bible very carefully, prayed in the middle of the night, slept on bare boards - as the novelist is quoted by Turnell - and would wash himself with cold water in winter as an act of merited penance. By the time of the emotional crisis involving his cousin, Gide had already experienced difficulties arising from his sexual behavior. When he was eight years old, the boy had been dismissed from school for an entire term because he had been observed masturbating in class. Indeed, the family doctor dealt with the difficult situation by threatening a surgical operation - as a cure. In the light of contemporary psychoanalytical awareness, one can only surmise what great damage might not have been inflicted by this **episode**, particularly for a boy who would lose his father three years later and who grew up in a manless household, in a repressive environment. When Gide was twelve years old, he was taken to Montpellier, at whose university his uncle, Charles Gide, was a professor of political economy. His Protestantism earned him numbers of jibes and taunts; he developed a nervous sickness, which shadowed his life for many years afterward. He eventually went to the Sorbonne - the University of Paris - but he never got a degree.

THE CAREER BEGINS

By the end of 1890, Gide had completed his book, *The Notebooks of André Walter*, for which few critics have claimed any literary merit. It was published in 1891. The book deals with the tension, which characterized the relationship between Gide and his surroundings. Gide wrote later, in 1926, that the book was really about the struggle to overcome masturbation, to which he had regressed in his twentieth year, at a time when he rejected the possibilities of ordinary sexual activities. The book sold extremely few copies - it had been published anonymously and privately. He had fond hopes for the volume, but the least of which included the wish that his cousin Madeleine would look upon him with greater favor after its publication and marry him. She did not, at this time, a refusal probably due to a series of domestic difficulties and her father's death at about this point in her life.

The failure of *The Notebooks of André Walter*, however, was not complete. Through his friend Pierre Louÿs the writer, Gide met Stéphane Mallarmé, the leading symbolist poet of the period, a man who elicited profound veneration from a number of writers among whom were to be found some of the future immortals of French letters. Mallarmé had a habit of holding soirées at his home every Tuesday, which Gide started to attend.

Mallarmé read the young man's book and complimented him on it. It was at such meetings that Gide met Paul Valéry, who was to become one of the most important French poets of the twentieth century. In 1893 Gide, with his friend Paul Albert Laurens - who was studying painting - went to North Africa. It was the first time the young man had quit the oppressive Protestant environment, which had so shaped his life, and he had a deep conviction of the importance of the trip. Feeling himself to be the divided plaything of obscure and powerful drives, he hoped that some organic oneness would be discovered in Africa. Jean Delay, in his biography *The Early Years of André Gide*, writes that the young man - who says in his autobiography that he was without his Bible for the first time - sent a letter to his mother asking her to send the Bible to a town in southern France. He refused to leave for Africa before it arrived. (This disclosure is cited by Turnell.) Gide had his first, sudden homosexual experience with an Arab child, after which he went to Biskra, where Laurens and he hired a prostitute, whom they shared. However, Gide started to spit blood; and Laurens, concerned about possible tuberculosis, got in touch with Mme. Gide, who came to Africa and discovered the situation. Although Gide told his mother that he and his companion were sharing the prostitute, Gide discloses in his *Journals* fifty years later that the situation was not a pleasant one, or a successful one. A doctor diagnosed Gide's pulmonary troubles as nervous and not tubercular, to Gide's immense relief. In 1895, Gide went to North Africa for the second time. Although he had originally wanted to go by himself, he got cold feet and wrote to his mother asking both her and Madeleine to come with him. He was refused. Possibly a fear of the repetition of what had occurred the previous time weighed him down, and the refusal freed him to attempt more experimentation. In January, he discovered that Oscar Wilde and Lord Alfred Douglas were staying at the same hotel in North Africa. Although Gide had met Wilde briefly in Paris, he had not known about Wilde's homosexuality at that time. At first, he wanted to leave the hotel immediately, erased his name from the register and went off to the station. On the way, he repented of his cowardice and returned. Apparently, the meetings later with Wilde and Douglas were among the most significant of Gide's entire life. From that time on, the novelist no longer looked upon his secret desires with loathing and fear. Gide started to develop into the assertive nonconformist who would alter the face of French letters.

EXALTATION AND CONSOLIDATION

Gide began a new book in North Africa, *Fruits of the Earth*, published in 1897. It celebrated the realities of joy, freedom and the flight from the repressions imposed by all the social forces, which impose restraints upon the growing self. The covering of habit patterns, duties and obligations, which conceal and suppress the real self must be broken through if life is to be made to yield the authentic satisfactions of which it is capable. Gide's mother died in 1895, and seventeen days after her death he became engaged to his cousin, whom he married in October 1895. Gide says in his *Journals* that upon his mother's death he experienced a mixture of love, distress and liberty. Critics have filled many pages in an attempt to explain to themselves and to their readers the reasons for Gide's marriage. The novelist himself discusses the question in his *Journals*, but his speculations do not lead to any fast conclusions. Guerard writes that Madeleine represented for Gide the powers of piety, which are manifested in both *The Immoralist* and *Strait Is the Gate*, and Gide himself has stated that all his books prior to 1926 were written under her influence. Turnell states that the marriage was not consummated during the honeymoon and quotes from an unpublished diary Gide wrote in 1896, in which the novelist mentions the number of times he confused Madeleine with his mother - a confusion which psychologists commonly point to as intimately allied with impotence. When Gide and Madeleine returned to France in 1806 he was elected mayor of the little town of La Roque-Baignard; he was then the youngest mayor in France.

Although *Fruits of the Earth* sold only five hundred copies in the ten-year period which followed its publication, it had an extraordinary appeal for the youth of France after the miserable debacles of the First World War.

GIDE THE NOVELIST

Although Gide experimented in various forms, he is by general consent at his best in narrative. Early attempts at some fictional achievements, like *The Notebooks of André Walter* and *Urien's Travels* (published in 1891 and 1893 respectively) were less fictional narratives involved with plot and character portrayal than examinations of reflexive moods and attitudes. In fact, a representative listing of Gide's works will feature these two volumes in a category entitled "Poetry in Verse and Prose" rather than a category of "Prose Fiction," for instance. Gide himself only called one of his fictions a novel, *The Counterfeiters*, published in 1926. He divided his narrative fictions into three general categories: novel, "récit," and "sotie." The second noun refers to such books as *The Immoralist* and *Strait Is the Gate*, as well as the *The Pastoral Symphony* (published in 1919) and the trilogy *Isabelle*, *Robert* and *Geneviève*. Gide has stated that all his narratives are ironic, involved with the essential discrepancies between individuals' senses of the world and what that world is like in a larger context. The "récit," always features a narrator, involved in the telling of bygone occurrences in his life - occurrences which have brought him to what is usually a moral impasse in the present. The two dimensions referred to above slowly impinge upon the reader's awareness. We first become absorbed in what the narrator is saying, and as we read - or upon a second reading - we discover the ironical dissimilarities between the narrator's "truth" and the encompassing reality which the "récit" as a whole communicates. These aspects of *The Immoralist* and *Strait Is the Gate* will become clear to the reader of this study when we examine two of the narratives in detail. The third category, that of the "soties," involves such works as *The Vatican Swindle* and *Prometheus Misbound*, books which may be described as satirical farces. In such narratives the novelist sacrifices conventional plot structure, and in its place utilizes diaries, speeches, dialogues. In addition Gide introduces sudden shifts in tone, levels of speech and mood. Thus the "soties" are written in a context whose exact tonality is difficult to establish, semi-farcical and quite serious and philosophical by turns. The technique of course is very much in keeping with the breaking down of established categories of "classical" traditions involving "tragic" and "comic" types of literature. As twentieth-century art and psychology and anthropology examined man and found in him a flux of contradictory impulses coexisting within one individual, the old rigidities of classification were subjected to considerable alterations. In comparison with the "soties," the "récits" have a more classical unity of plot and process, a greater emphasis upon investigation of character. Between 1909 and 1926 Gide became an important public figure. Impelled by his new self-confidence and the urgings of his puritan conscience he published in 1924 a book entitled *Corydon*, which was a frank statement of his homosexual sympathies, as well as a defense of such inclinations. By the time Gide published *The Counterfeiters* in 1926 he was ready to give up the first-person narrative and its attendant intimacy - attributes of the earlier "récits." Ironically, it is the "récits," which, according to a large number of critics, may survive longer than others of Gide's narrations. *The Counterfeiters* has been compared with the novels of Proust and Joyce, which also appeared in the 1920's; but time has not been favorable to such a verdict. *The Counterfeiters* has been defined by the critic Henri Peyre as "a novelist writing a novel about a novelist trying to write a novel." The novel is less the presentation of complex and full-bodied characters acting within a conventional fictional framework than it is an exercise in the meaning of honesty, an investigation in the myriad possibilities for self-delusion.

GIDE FROM 1914

Upon the outbreak of the First World War, Gide helped found an organization for assisting Belgian refugees. But within a couple of years he was back at his home in the country, Cuverville, busy writing. Gide by this time had been in the habit of making many trips with Henri Ghéon, a minor writer. Madeleine, who was accustomed to opening those of Gide's letters which came from certain friends, discovered the truth about Gide and his sexual proclivities in no ambiguous manner from one of these letters. Whether she had known or not, whether she had had strong suspicions or not, this letter was a shock to her. At the same time Gide was experiencing a religious conflict. According to some writings of this period it appears that Gide was considering conversion to Catholicism. (In 1949 the correspondence between Gide and a fervently Catholic poet and dramatist, Paul Claudel, was published, bearing witness to the intensity of the exchange of ideas between the two men between 1899 and 1926-an exchange significantly concerned with the merits of the Church as spiritual home.) In any case Gide never became a convert, and eventually broke off relations with Claudel, whose early work he had helped launch in the *Nouvelle Revue Française*, a magazine which Gide founded with some friends in 1908. In 1917 Gide and a young friend, Marc Allégret, voyaged to England for a period of four months. His wife, discovering that her husband was not making the trip alone, reacted strongly. He wrote her a letter the night before departure, in which he said that he was rotting in her presence. When he returned he was greeted by the discovery that Madeleine had burned all his letters. *Corydon* - mentioned previously - was published in 1924, although written in 1916, and *If It Die*, Gide's frank autobiography, in 1926. Although he received the Nobel Prize in 1947, his most significant work was behind him by the time the 1930's opened. In 1926 and 1927, as a result of his visits to the Congo, he published *Travels in the Congo*. In 1929 he published *The School for Wives*, and in 1929 and 1936 the two succeeding "récits" in the series, *Robert* and *Geneviève*, works from which the old intensity and originality have departed. After visits to the Soviet Union he wrote two small volumes, *Return from the USSR* and *Afterthoughts on the USSR*, in 1936 and 1937, generally rather negative about an experience he had had more hopes for.

Madeleine died in 1938. During the war Gide spent most of his time in Unoccupied France, some of it in North Africa, where he began a new magazine *L'Arche* and did relatively little writing of any significance. When he died in Paris in 1951 he was buried next to his wife in a Protestant ceremony, although he had left instructions that his remains be cremated. There was actually a dispute in the churchyard between various factions, one of which wanted to observe his intent to the letter.

THE IMMORALIST

. . . .

ONE

The letter

Opening *The Immoralist* with a letter, apparently written by one of Michel's friends to Mr. D. R., the Prime Minister, is quite in keeping with Gide's general position in his fictions. The reader learns that the book is made up of an oral narration by a man speaking to friends of his schooldays and youth. We also learn that Michel apparently occupies a privileged position in French society, since the letter is addressed to a person in a high position, who can be written to rather informally, though in a tone of respectful detachment. We learn a few details of Michel's life and realize that his friends are very concerned for his well-being. The great need, apparently is for an appropriate position in which Michel could forget his haunting dilemma, or at least into which he could funnel the self-lacerating energies which have been set in motion by the happenings of which we are promised the details later in the body of the book.

The beginning

Like almost all of Gide's main characters, Michel is the product of the upper-middle Protestant classes of France. It is almost immediately apparent that whatever tension the book will hold will proceed from the internal conflict within the character rather than from the unrolling of a traditionally directed plot structure. Note that the placement of father and mother in this first section of the First Part is exactly the opposite of what happened in Gide's own life - he was a boy of eleven when his father died; he became engaged within three weeks of his mother's death. In spite of this rather symmetrical transparent alteration of his own history, Gide did make *The Immoralist* one of his most clearly autobiographical narratives. Significantly Michel does not describe the father. He is a scholar, but we never find out exactly what kind, where he works or teaches, what books he might have written. We do learn that Michel was quite astounded to discover after his father's death that his fortune was extensive. The son and his father had led such a gravely renunciatory life that considerations of finance, beyond necessities, had never come up.

The narrative style, supposedly that of a man talking to sympathetic friends, does not manifest the colloquial qualities which a reader might expect. Rather we find that Michel's speech is decorous, detached and perfectly syntactical, attributes of written prose more than of spontaneous speaking. Thus the reader is led by means of the style itself to an appreciation of Michel's position as speaker. The story he tells, though apparently loaded with moral complexities, is conveyed by a person who seems to be constructing an almost "artistic" pattern as he remembers and talks. Such a pattern cannot help falsifying the truth of experience. Obviously even an unsyntactical, hurried or emotionally unbound delivery does not guarantee the communication of the "truth." But the studied artificiality of Michel's speech carries us a clear distance away from the firsthand relation of painful material. The distance of Michel's character, with its suggestion of narrative obtuseness, will become more and more important.

In this first section of the First Part Michel reveals both an extraordinary naïveté and a very childish pettiness and disregard for other people's feelings. The reader becomes aware directly of the intensely narcissistic dimensions of Michel's character. His training and education in Protestant "self-discipline" and suppression of personal concern, the reverse side of the infantile rage which characterizes his statement to Marceline, already comes into significant focus in this section. His initial impulse to keep the truth from his wife was in the tradition of what he was taught as noble and self-denying; the later self-pity was the result of a personality straining against an overly powerful sense of self-suppression.

TWO

The absolutist

A very important aspect of Michel's character is brought out in this section. He looses all his frustration and anger directly at his wife, as if she is to blame for his situation. The curve of his temperamental reactions to Marceline is similar in this section to that which we have seen in the first, but here it is intensified by his craving for life and the sudden intrusion of the symbol of rejuvenation - the young Arab boy Bachir. The behavioral pattern very much recalls that of a small child in relation to its mother. The characteristic aspect of such a relationship involves the extremes of dependency and rebellion, neither of which comes about from a stable or mature character. Sickness, particularly severe sickness, commonly reduces adults to such a state. But tuberculosis is by no means the exclusive agent for Michel's narcissistic ploys. His illness serves as a go-between, temporarily justifying his immature irrationalities and self-absorption. And it is the reader's awareness of the psychological effects of illness which make him accept without much impatience Marceline's unresisting acceptance of Michel's impositions. At this point in the narrative, her behavior does not necessarily suggest an unnaturally selfless human being.

The symbolic value of Bachir, brief as his appearance is, pervades the entire section. The first instances of sensuality proceeding from Michel are directed not at his wife but toward Bachir. Now all these reactions are interpreted by Michel as upsurges of love for life, results of the frustrations at the limitations imposed by his illness. Psychiatrists have stated that tuberculosis can have a neurotic origin. It is perhaps not too much to entertain the possibility that Michel's spasm occurred as the result of unreconciled inner tension. He has no awareness of the real cause of the attraction which the boy holds for him, yet the pull of this attraction is inextricably involved with Michel's desperate desire for health. A further **irony** in this anthology of ironies makes its brief appearance and passes without making any heavy-handed overt claims on the reader's attention, but will in retrospect impose its importance - Marceline's role. In view of the primarily platonic aspect of their relationship up to this time, the very observant reader may experience a transistory wonder at the possible dark sources which motivate her action. To what degree is Marceline herself interested in maintaining an obstacle to a closer intimacy between herself and her husband? Such questions, the germinating suggestions of the narrative, hardly come into focus at this point largely because of the skill with which Gide lightly grazes each potentially symbolic incident. Gide is unwilling for artistic reasons to emphasize any stage of development lest he lose the realistic and progressive patina of **realism** which, in fact, deluded most of the early readers of this book, few of whom glimpsed the essential sexual nature of the action and the conflicts.

THREE

Bashour and the shawl

The tone for this section is set by Michel's comments about his body. It is a plea for the easy way out, rationalized here, and justified by the conditions of illness - as Michel's separation from his wife was justified previously by the more critical stage of his illness. Michel's attentions to the Arab boys partake only of sensual dimensions. What attracts him to Ashour? No more than he had in Bachir did Michel find, or seek, in Ashour any particular attribute of personality. What he found, and reacted to, was pure physical presence, a skin tone, a symbol of health - in other words, he sought only what he wanted for himself.

Another interesting clue to Michel's state at this time is suggested by his fear of Marceline's disapproval of Ashour. Why was he worried? Clearly, although unconscious of his progressive inner developments, Michel was experiencing some of the claims of buried Protestant conscience. Rather than acknowledge their presence in himself, he projected their demands onto his wife, who more and more becomes the scapegoat of his psychic life. Although he is irritated by his misconception of Marceline's probable reaction, he is able to notice one aspect of Marceline's relationship to this scrawny little boy she is helping out. And of course it is her maternal propensities of which he becomes aware, a reaction completely consistent with the lineaments of their mutual bonds. The sensual gratifications he experiences in the presence of Bachir and Ashour, which he cannot feel with his wife, he also exults in. The garden scene is presented so artfully that the action - conceivably a neutral demonstration of sensuality - becomes invested with the overtones of self-serving narcissism. The constricting Puritanism of his upbringing loosens for the first time to allow entrance to long-lost activities of sense and memory. The reader of Gide recalls at this juncture the ecstatic greetings to nature which pervade *If It Die*.

FOUR

Marceline and the boys

In this section the seductions represented by the world of the Arab boys become more and more apparent. Though the writing remains clearly in the realistic tradition, the reader senses with growing conviction that every phrase, every act, may embody significant symbolic meanings. The very road, for instance, which Marceline has discovered and on which she leads Michel at the beginning of this section, suggests an interior journey.

But there is another conflict within Michel, beyond the growing competition in his mind between Marceline and the boys Lassif, Lachmi and Moktir. Marceline has her own favorites among the young Arabs. Michel reacts to them without any effort to analyze his motivations; they breed in him irritation, almost disgust and fear. As the unconscious material in his personality occupies more waking time and makes increasing demands

Michel reacts angrily to the boys who are Marceline's favorites. He sees them as embodiments of attitudes which he must at all costs transcend, symbolic threats to his burgeoning sensuality. And Marceline herself, by extension, becomes increasingly part of the potentially repressive world of his past.

The incident of Moktir's theft solidifies Michel's rebellious tendencies. He abdicates his position as a mature, responsible adult and actively joins the dark underworld of his urges as embodied by the young robber. Michel consciously accepts his positive celebration of hedonism and lawlessness. More than the theft itself, it was the boy's betrayal of Marceline's faith which appealed to Michel, unable to betray her himself, but quite ready to embrace Moktir's symbolic action as representative of his own inclinations. This silent complicity is the initial step in Michel's active dissociation from his wife. And it is a complicity, we must not forget, within the context of childish cunning; it does not by itself reduce the implicit power of Marceline's pious devotions; in fact it forces Marceline increasingly into the position of moral judge, representative of spiritual sanctions, at the same time as it makes of Michel himself a "criminal."

FIVE

The swollen stems

Critics have used the term "pathetic fallacy" to denote the attribution to nature of vegetative changes sympathetic with an individual's emotions. Nineteenth-century Romantic literature in France demonstrates a good number of instances of this "fallacy," by means of which the natural world serves as mirror and symbol of personal human feelings. The most powerful description of natural scenes in this section recalls to the reader man's persistence in perceiving unnatural processes the external manifestation of his own preoccupations. The land is waking from its dormant period, filled to bursting with sap and urgings. The reader will remember that all details are chosen by the narrator, Michel, and the phallic suggestiveness of his descriptions admirably directs our attention to the narrator's unconscious concerns. His experience of life-giving forces extends to an appreciation of his wife's aloneness. In conformity with the suggestions implicit in Michel's sense of the natural environment, he decides he needs something new.

The reader, profiting from his special perspective, can analyze Michel's insomnia. This fever of life may just as reasonably be related to intense anxiety. Michel is in the grip of a terrible fear of death, possibly the result of his partial awareness that he is daring his concealed self to show itself; that the coming trip might reveal a buried Michel, whose manifestations would have to incur the most severe punishment by the traditional forces of morality in him, whose power he had known only too well. In order to combat this terrifying sense of foreboding he seeks to prove to himself that he is alive. But he feels a dread sense of oncoming feebleness and advancing age.

SIX

A palimpsest

The artificial divorce between soul and body continues. The improvement in Michel's health does not serve as a reason for the reconstitution of his increasingly split self. The great fact is that Michel feels his post-sickness self, new as it may be, is a real and basic alteration of his personality. Michel's reference to a palimpsest, an old text on parchment or tablet under which the investigator may discover a yet older text, not quite rubbed out or erased, has significance. The psychology here is somewhat elementary, as if the human personality is reduced in complexity to some kind of nut or vegetable, layered evenly, and subject to being stripped down to the basic kernel or seed. The overlays which Michel conceives of as pernicious include his learning, his ethical inheritance, his love of history. Here again, as in several former situations, we are confronted by the problem of the quality of Michel's free will. We must never forget that he is addressing his talk to his friends, that man - however "honest" - always seeks self-justification. Michel's state, in general, is not that of a man easily able to make his own determinations or to impose his own will. He has only a very limited insight into his own motivations. And those occasional perceptions which he does not describe are never placed into a continuous or temperamentally informative context. Michel has experienced a thrill of complicity with the theft, yet the acknowledgement of the momentary sensation of pleasure is all he allows himself. Far from allowing his new self to blossom out in its own good time, Michel is very busy repressing the potential activity of his intelligence and of his analytical capacities. His self-praising recollections insist on some character traits which have already been apparent in any context until now: patience, and cooperation. A rebuttal might suggest that although Michel is incapable of these character traits in connection with others, his intense narcissism certainly permits him to pay concentrated attention to himself. Michel's "free will" is a retrogressive abstention from any ethical involvements as they relate to any other person. His pleasures are almost never shared; in fact the presence of his wife or even of some of the boys, in this section, is in opposition to his wishes.

SEVEN

Narcissus

The only important action in this section involves Michel's visit to the barber. His first feeling, apparently, was fear not pleasure. He speculates that the reason, the real reason for his fear, had to do with the sudden stripping-down of his mind. The sequence, typically brief, nevertheless is very suggestive. It includes inconsistencies, and rationalizations. For Michel has been at great pains to deny the reality and the workings of the mind for some time now. In this very section he discloses his disgust at the scholarly, studious past which the beard had come to symbolize. It is not his mind which he greets with the combination of recognition, fear and delight; it is the body. Ironically the quality of this veneration equals the intensity of his former commitments. This conscientious puritan, in the process of detaching himself from his former overzealous archaeological activities, is carrying over into his new self the same devoted absolutism which seems more and more to denote an essential aspect of his personality. In fact Michel's self-involvement is nothing new. From what the reader has been able to gather, Michel's earlier life had been as gross an exercise in isolating self-involvement as his vaunted new existence. The significant difference, of course, lies in the fact that formerly his concerns could be directed outward, toward ancient texts, drawings, scholarly books; his intent now is to study and regenerate himself, exclusively. This exclusivity and self-absorption result in some remarkable statements, whose profound irrationality could only be missed by the speaker himself. In his comments about his wife, we are faced then, in an effort to make some kind of understandable sense of these inconsistencies, with a possible definition of "love" which may fit the contexts in which the word is used by Michel. What does he mean by "love"?

Obviously he cannot mean a relationship between a man and a woman in which attempts at honesty in each inform the quality of the communication between the two. What is the quality of Marceline's love for her husband? If the illusory being who was the object of her love could so alter in his attitude to himself - and to her - without her noticing, one might think that her own love was so detached from reality as to make a fitting analogue to his narcissism. As a matter of fact, Michel's own sense of a growing dissimulation as regards his wife may in itself be an illusion. In no significant way had he been emotionally connected with her previously, so that his appreciation of his present distance takes on the quality of sophistry. We ask again about the kind of love to which Michel refers in this section. The only answer is "self-love." Psychology has for decades now observed some interesting relationships among narcissism, homosexuality, regression and sexual attraction to young children. These matters are extremely complex, obscure and contentious, but their **exposition** in this book must certainly be interesting and provocative to the reader.

EIGHT

The coachman and Marceline

This section is a beautiful example of self-deception. The significant **episode** is completely misconceived. All of Michel's talk ignores the palpable fact that it is precisely because of the assault, and the sexual activity which the attack promoted, that Michel is able for the first time to function as a lover. A superficial reading of this section would agree with Michel's interpretation of the events and of the moods following the event. For what is dearer to woman than a knight on a white charger, or lacking that, at least a courageous avenger? And what is more pleasant to a man than the unbounded admiration of a woman for his masculine exploits, her praise coming just at the time that his convalescence permits him to assume the conventional role of husband? But all these explanations, implicit in Michel's relation of the story, fail to satisfy the careful reader. They fail to satisfy the need for coherence and developmental continuity. In this section particularly, we are aware of the very careful, classical narrative structure observed by the author. In fact the irritating and upsetting intimacies of revelation implied by the narrative action require, in this very early twentieth-century book, the detached and carefully worked style which characterizes it. Or at the very least Gide required such a style, for he was, to a very large degree, a classicist whose path toward free expression of tabooed materials and "libertine" rebellions went against the grain.

Perhaps the most self-deluded passage in this section appears in Michel's "romantic" fin-de-siècle lamentation over the ephemeral aspects of love. He, the singer of the body, of pure sensuality, absorbing self-interest, now sings the sad false song of **metaphysical** regret. It is almost as if the concept of "soul" serves as a handy verbal counter, loaded with all its literary and predetermined associations, ready to fit in to rationalizing banalities. Michel is utterly unable to face the reality of his impotence, and romanticizes the one intimacy which accident had made possible.

The undercurrents of his situation suggest that his tears may be tears of pleasure, or fearful anticipation that his wife might begin to demand something from him. The reader can only praise the dexterity with which Gide in such a section as this is able to communicate the surface of truth while drawing up from the deeps the fear-inducing possibilities of Michel's avoidances.

NINE

The end of the beginning

This section ends the first of the three important divisions of the book, the First Part.

The significance of Michel's choice of the Goths and, more particularly, King Athalaric cannot be easily missed. Its profounder meaning lies in Michel's decision to find in his scholarly work an analogue of his seductive personal concerns. By such a decision he automatically ties his past life to his present alterations. In addition he exposes, in however masked a form, his new involvements to the world. Michel's decision thus is the next symbolic incident in the developmental curve which began with his initial sickness. But although Michel readily accepts the fact that it is Athalaric's "barbaric" attitude which so attracts him, he does his best to read a moral lesson in the young Goth's early and horrible death. There is an interesting double suggestion here. On the one hand we perceive the still-powerful influence of Michel's Protestantism acting in the old patterns of sermonizing symbolism - although by now, we can no longer be sure of Michel's complete conscious honesty toward his friends. On the other hand we may assume that the young Athalaric also represents for Michel those aspects of the unexplainable in the future which Michel must transcend.

The reader expects that the hedonistic self-absorbed activities of Michel will continue, or at least find an appropriate environment for their further elaboration. It is clear that the city/country split will acquire symbolic value, particularly in view of Michel's lyrical reminiscences of the large pleasant house, the running streams, the greenery...for we know by now that very little is wasted in this book. And indeed critics have pointed out how every passage, every phrase, even particular words are chosen with extreme artistic care by Gide, who is intent on making this "récit" as tightly bound a structure as possible. Even the epigraph to the entire book is significant, and can be applied now, as we have come to the end of the First Part. The epigraph is a quotation from the Old Testament Psalm 139: "I will praise thee; for I am fearfully and wonderfully made." The peculiar appositeness of "fear" and "wonder" as they apply to Michel's attempts to continue his bewildered wanderings needs no elaboration.

THE IMMORALIST

SECOND PART

....

ONE

La Morinière

Michel feels more and more confident. The processes of vegetative growth move him to considerations of order and reconstruction. But soon his old absolutist tendencies reveal themselves even in his private speculations. The value of these speculations for the reader lies in their communication of Michel's intense belief in the intelligence and the processes of rationality - thoughts at the other pole from the happy hedonism with which he had amused himself in Africa. Interestingly, as the section comes to an end, Michel discovers that Bocage, whom he had implicitly trusted, was perhaps not so efficient as he had believed.

The entire section ends on a note of disappointment. The reader learns, too, that Michel's interest in the lands does not emanate from his personal concern for these matters. He becomes involved in them through Charles. In fact, we see in this friendship a repetition of previous situations. At first, Marceline's announcement moves her husband to great emotion and a short period of great closeness with her. But the arrival of Charles distracts Michel again from the attention to and concern for his wife. It is a distraction which uses as its rationale Michel's growing interest in the farm and the livestock and the tenant farmers.

The sensual high point in this long section does not involve Michel and his wife any more than it has involved them at any previous time. Nor does it relate to Michel's apprehension of nature. It comes up in relation to Bocage's son, Charles. In general Charles is presented as the intermediary between Michel and nature. What Michel on his own responded to was the memory of the past.

TWO

Ménalque

The focal center of this section is, of course, the older homosexual Ménalque. He represents the outlaw from society, the man who has chosen not to attempt a life of bourgeois respectability. Critics have complained that this character and his lengthy discourses are flaws in the structure of this novel. And there is no doubt that the long conversations between him and Michel seem **didactic** in a way that has not been true of the rest of the book. The reader will recall, from the Introduction to this Study Guide, Gide's meeting with Oscar Wilde in Africa, Gide's high vulnerability to that confrontation, his fears and doubts, the attitude of Wilde. This character Ménalque - probably based on

Wilde - plays a crucial part here as well. Michel reacts to him as to an awe-inspiring reference point of profound perceptions.

As the older man, Ménalque has the advantage. He perceives the conflicts in Michel's personality, aware of them through his knowledge of their similarity to his own. But he has resolved them in his own fashion. And since Michel is constantly prey to confusion and lack of self-knowledge, he confers an almost godly status upon Ménalque. The symbolic relationship between the two men is accentuated by a plot element smacking a little of the old-fashioned intrusion of "coincidence." From this point on we may almost say that Michel's marriage is at an end. By the end of this section he looks at Marceline, for all his apparent love and concern and guilt, as stained and diseased. And for Michel disease and ill health carry **connotations** which are unbearable. Like most narcissists he is essentially concerned with his own body and his own self; the possibility of their disintegration, of their subjection to temporal processes cannot be borne. Thus growth for Michel, which implies also aging, carries with it all kinds of implicit threats. This attitude has already been demonstrated by his reactions to the vegetation both in Africa and in La Morinière. He could not enjoy the patterns of growth, decay and rebirth for themselves. In Africa the lush landscapes and oases were merely mirrors in which he could see reflected the continuity of his cares about himself. In La Morinière the beauty of the Norman woods and livestock and fish and water became the objects of a contemplation which ended in daydreams of some sort of impossible perfectibility. Michel cannot take anything in the world as it is.

Nothing pleases Michel. Nobody passes his rigorous tests. No situation yields any pleasantness. No comradeship is possible. Throughout this section Michel contemptuously dismisses the social evenings - salons - for their frivolity and repetitive dullness. Nobody understands him, and none can be expected to. Again the worth of individuals is measured by the degree to which they serve his own purposes. Unable to go toward others, he grows furious when they will not come gratuitously toward him. Even his professional colleagues, archaeologists and philologists, give him no pleasure. He goes further and attempts to find some hope in relationships with poets and novelists. But here too the sense is that they only consider living as an irritating barrier to the act of writing. Philosophers - for he goes through an extensive list of possibilities - are no better. That Marceline should finally join the grand parade of the rejected is hardly a surprise. In fact it is almost unusual that his detachment from and distaste for her should have taken so long to crystallize. The demon of self-love, allied with the gnawings of confusion and the fear of unconscious demands, is more and more ready to take over, dashing Michel's pious hopes for any sort of stability.

THREE

The disintegration

The controlling images and events in this section are those of disintegration. Two primary manifestations define the tone of this section: Michel's feeling about the fields, and Michel's attitude toward the young men.

The wounded field. Michel indicates that his main feeling is a kind of perverse pleasure. It is not clear how far some of the symbolism in this section is to be taken as applicable to the thematic bases of the narrative; but we may make some attempt at reading it. Heurtevent, for instance, is a combination of a form of the verb heurter, which means "to knock against" or "to slam" (also used figuratively, in which case it generally

28

means "to wound") and of the noun vent which means "wind." Perhaps we may see in the old timber merchant an embodiment of those impersonal and brutish forces in the universe which Michel finds so sympathetic. We will recall Michel's interest in the young Gothic king, whose ruthless barbarism undercut the sophistication of his civilized training, and Michel's profound involvement in the antisocial self as represented by Moktir, Ménalque and Alcide. In addition, we may also see in the tardy removal of the tree trunks and the destruction of the young shoots the corruption of the young and rising life - although doomed in some instances - through the wounds of older and dead organic material. Again this is a possible **metaphor** relevant to Michel's sense of the need for a progressive stripping-down of the old self and its habits.

The young men. As Michel progressively discovers the secret lives of the peasants, the reader senses these discoveries essentially as equivalent to Michel's own voyages inside himself. As far as Marceline is concerned, Michel's last-minute passionate worry about her health is transparently hypocritical. What he needs to do is to escape from a farm which he himself has turned into a living **metaphor** of guilt, disease and fear. He feels overwhelmed and speaks of his love as a frightened boy talks to a sick mother whose comfort he needs and whose moral attitude he rebels against.

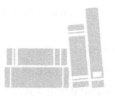

THE IMMORALIST

THIRD PART

. . . .

ONE

The end

This final section of the book is terrible in its precipitous decline into death. Michel's brutality toward his wife constantly cloaks itself as concern. His passionate outcries of worry and love reveal themselves more and more clearly as merely impatience at the slowness of Marceline's decline. The rank waste of his capital is a partial expiation for what is nothing less than his murder of Marceline; and in addition there is a kind of race between the rapid financial (and moral) denudation of Michel and the hour of his wife's death, almost as if he were asking her to die before he was completely without money.

But the reader gleans from Michel's attitude toward his wife a ghastly portrait of Michel unwilling to let her out of his sight, waiting for her death, masquerading as the heartsick lover.

The peculiar and dark ambiguity of the narrative takes its coloring partly from the narrator's continued self-delusion about his characteristic desires. Now he is unable to move; he is emotionally paralyzed. The freedom for which he had pined so intensely is now his, hanging around his conscience like a band of death. What is he to do? How can these friends help him? What atonement is possible? And aside from all these questions, the reader keeps asking himself whether Michel has grown in self-awareness to any discernible degree. This lack of self-knowledge is perhaps the most grotesque and frightful aspect of the narrative.

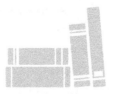

THE IMMORALIST

. . . .

MICHEL

The essential and significant aspects of Michel's character are perceived by the reader in the course of slow and crystallizing revelations, communicated by the formal narrative means chosen by Gide. Michel is the first person narrator, and as such reveals himself and the true quality of his activities only indirectly. For all his apparent attempts to speak honestly to his friends, the reader is constantly aware - if he is concentrating on his reading - that no man is free from the absolute need for self-justification. Man is an animal that seeks for reasons. We, the readers, can never discover what has actually happened to Michel. The main **themes** of Michel's life, as we read of them, include a number of basic problems common to twentieth-century literature: the quest for identity, the search for authenticity, the puzzling makeup of individual psychological structures, the return of the repressed, the outsider and his relationship to the established orders, the latent destructiveness of human beings. It is not possible to read of Michel's eventual dilemma without experiencing the sense of alienation and horror, and occasionally the thrill of sympathy.

MARCELINE

She is Michel's wife, characterized primarily by an absolutely extraordinary tendency toward self-immolation. At no point in the book, even when she is in peril of her life, does she put forth objections motivated by her instinct for self-preservation. In fact, this instinct, supposedly basic and universal in mankind, is almost totally absent in her. Although represented as a figure of extreme spirituality and delicacy, she communicates to the reader a sense of almost pathological self-denial. She is probably subject to self-delusions even more marked than those which afflict her husband. She makes no demands upon him, and her final inexorable journey toward death elicits from her - according to Michel - not one serious remonstrance. Again the problem of form brings the reader up short. To what degree are we to conceive Marceline as she is presented? How much of the story has Michel consciously or unconsciously fabricated in order to preserve some self-justification? We will of course never be able to establish conclusions. But no doubt the essentials of her character would not be significantly different from those which are presented to us. Her role in this book is like an inversely proportional barometer. She declines as he becomes progressively subject to the inhuman, demonic powers that make him insist to her that the weak have no excuse for living.

MÉNALQUE

Probably influenced by Gide's personal memory of Oscar Wilde, with perhaps an admixture of Nietzsche, this character symbolizes the hedonist, antisocial, self-absorbed man. His role in the narrative is essentially catalytic. He plays no real part in the unrolling plot continuity of the book, but the shadow of his philosophy and the dark imprint of his spirit haunt Michel's comings and goings. The fact that Ménalque is presented as both an outcast (rendered one by his own desires) and a successful diplomatic courier is of great importance to Michel who, confused about his own identity, finds in the older man a seductive and possible model.

MOKTIR

A young Arab boy whose presence in the home of the convalescent Michel helps to initiate the downward path of Michel's inclinations.

BOCAGE

This caretaker, or bailiff, of Michel's farm, tends to represent the more or less "normal" aspects of the rooted peasant life whose continuity, for all of its secret decadence, contrasts radically with the rootlessness and directionless voyagings of the young protagonist.

ALCIDE

Bocage's younger son.

BUTE

The head of the timber workers' team.

HEURTEVENT

The timber merchant. He plays a rather symbolic role, in that he is the agent directly responsible for the death of young trees. Like Ménalque he is less an integral part of the plot than a figure representative of certain profound tendencies in Michel's character.

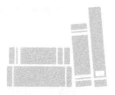

STRAIT IS THE GATE

. . . .

THE PROTESTANT BACKGROUND

The scene in the beginning of this narrative is set in the usual repressive and austerely religious Protestant French background typical of Gide's "récits." We note the interesting similarity in plot structure to that of *The Immoralist*. Within the first few pages of the book the reader immediately perceives the repressive atmosphere of the house where Jérôme lives. Though set in vegetative environment the home - described at length - communicates the constricting presence of walls surrounding it. Jérôme's natural inclinations, directed by the austere influences of his mother and Miss Ashburton, symbolized by the brooding reality of the house's walls, go automatically to Alissa.

The only figure in Part I whose essential attitude differs largely from the attitudes of the other characters is Lucile Bucolin, the wife of Michel's uncle. She represents the breath of hedonism, set against the Protestant middle-class values of her environment. Indeed, she comes from a West Indian family - another instance, like that involving the Arab boys in *The Immoralist*, of sun-drenched lands representing freedom from repressions and austerities. In Jérôme's recollections Lucile is a languid, lazy woman living in a kind of continual torpor. We find in Jérôme a variation of the prototype - so clearly exemplified in Michel of *The Immoralist* - whose self-denying and puritan tendencies match in rigor the power of the repressed and unconscious urges pressing in from below.

It is quite in order that the agent which moved Jérôme to his conception of heroic and virtuous devotion to Alissa should have been Minister Vautier. Christ's words, "Strive to enter in at the strait [narrow] gate," fills young Jérôme with the exaltation of religious renunciation. The promptings of his nature were reinforced by the minister's pointed sermon, for there was no doubt that his text meant that the hedonists who passed through the "wide gate" should be branded as traitors to religious injunctions.

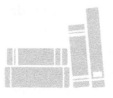

STRAIT IS THE GATE

PART II

THE IMPORTANCE OF JULIETTE

In this section Juliette, Alissa's sister, suddenly takes on a new importance. Although she is not directly involved in the essential "events" of the plot, she is a reference point around which the motivations and actions of both Alissa and Jérôme revolve. The configuration allows the reader to obtain a greater grasp of the situations.

To the degree that Alissa is a replacement for Jérôme's mother, to this degree is their relationship constrained, etherealized and unreal. We already know that this relationship is devoid of the sensual, heterosexual urgings which motivate poor Juliette. In this section it is the pathetic reality of this triangle, so unaware of itself for the most part, which gives Juliette her importance and increases the tension.

Alissa's letter to Jérôme, which is quoted in full in the text, is brief, cryptic and curious. She addresses Jérôme as if insisting upon the Platonic, spiritualized essence of their understanding.

STRAIT IS THE GATE

. . . .

PART III

THE DUTCH PEASANT CAP

Since no touch, however small, in Gide's, "récits" is absolutely random, we may recognize in the brief mention of an article of dress a symbolic reference, perhaps two symbolic references. In the first instance, the reader will notice the extraordinary appropriateness of the verb "to frame." We saw in Part I that the repressive physical environment of the Bucolin house constituted a material parallel to the constrictions of spirit within which Jérôme was growing up. We are now able to see even more clearly how powerfully Alissa is enclosed within her concepts of duty and the seductions of her devotional ideas of the after-life.

In the second place, the impression of Alissa's face disappearing within the depths of the great cap she wears underlines the degree to which she is retreating from the challenges of life and loving as they are posed by Jérôme. It is ironical that it should be he who represents the call of life, since he also finds renunciation seductive and cannot make a real break from his familial tradition. But the comparison between Alissa and Jérôme grants to the young man a greater capacity for life, even if his love for Alissa translates itself by a stated desire that his one desire is that his mind should differ in no way from hers.

A FURTHER IRONY

Abel Vautier plays in this section an interesting double role. He is at once more perceptive than Jérôme about Juliette, and he is also unable to see some aspects of the truth any more clearly than the other young man. He observes that the pigeonhole into which Juliette has been placed by Jérôme is inappropriate. He appreciates her sensitivity, her learning, her joyous love of life. His own involvement with his newly found love blinds him to the real reasons for Juliette's excessive excitement during the visit of the two young men. The ironies and the pathos of the now four-sided group are intensified by Abel's exuberant pronouncements at the end of Part III. His plans for the future, under ordinary circumstances, might be seen as the customary excesses of a young man in love, unaware of the complexities of the world and of its rigorous difficulties. And the more he talks, the more his pathetic volubility implants in the reader a growing awareness of man's capacity for self-delusion.

STRAIT IS THE GATE

. . . .

THE QUALITY OF RENUNCIATION

The triggering activity in Part IV is Alissa's perverse behavior, which is revealed in a series of discrete touches reminiscent of a detective story. The significance of the revelations grow progressively greater as the pace steps up. The possibility that Jérôme has been deluding himself about the quality of the relationship occurs to him, but he consciously suppresses his suspicions. The narrative suspense is kept at a high pitch by Aunt Plantier's innocent and deluded intervention. The reader wonders about the reasons for Alissa's ambivalent attitudes.

What are Alissa's motivations? How pure are they? To what degree is she aware of the intense suffering she is causing so many people? Could she, remaining true to her feelings, yet have acted in such a way that others' sensibilities could have been spared? At this stage of the narrative such questions are very difficult to answer in any definitive manner. We are faced by a number of perverse and ambiguous actions whose motivations cannot become too clear since we cannot share Alissa's thought processes; it is after all Jérôme who tells us all we can ever know. We have been given hints of her extraordinary austerity and detachment. At this point the reader senses that she may still go one of two ways: life may yet, in all its unexpectedness, pull her to a consideration of marriage and familial habitation; or she may go further in the direction of self-abnegation. Her ambiguous and imprecise actions - a little bit of "yes," a little piece of "no," a suggestion of "maybe" - may be due to a profound restlessness in her, a lack of clarity as to her own direction and her own real feelings. Is the feeling for her father a source of her behavior? Or could it be a rationalizing mask which covers up a certain taste for the sadistic manipulation of those individuals, like Jérôme, who see in her an unbelievably delicate self in whose presence mention of brutal realities (like marriage) seems inappropriate? The reader, juggling with all these possibilities, is made uncomfortable, cannot find solid ground, doubts his own perceptions, wishes he had more information. And it is this very desire for more specific information that points up the formal usefulness of the first-person narrator technique. Had this narrative been written in the manner common during the nineteenth century, the author would have assumed the omnipotent attitude, knowing and communicating to the reader the inmost activities of every important character's thought processes. But here, as in life, we can judge only through the medium of one individual's perceptions. And the psychological authenticity of this mode of perception cannot be lost upon people living in the psychoanalytic age of the twentieth century.

STRAIT IS THE GATE

PART V

....

YES AND NO

Part V provides no significantly new information which would enable the reader to judge better the particular quality of Alissa's motivations. She, in fact, only increases the degree of almost absurd inconsistency manifest in the correspondence. Only one individual in the entire panoply of characters in this section is able to look upon the scene, or any part of it, with any perspective of humor. That is Abel Vautier. He demonstrates his capacity for humor on several occasions.

For Jérôme, as for Alissa, if somewhat less, life is real, life is earnest. The liberating quality of laughter is absent from their oppressive style of life. They sense reality as a kind of sacred, renunciatory Protestant world of value whose utter sobriety restricts the free expression of feeling. This restriction masquerades as delicacy, concern, spiritual devotion, but not for all the members of the little society which with we have become acquainted in this book. Aunt Plantier, for instance, is able to express her concerns rather directly; what vitiates her possible importance is that her perception is not subtle enough to understand the folie-à-deux of Alissa and Jérôme. (A folie-à-deux is a shared illusion, within which individuals share an unspoken, and to some degree unaware, agreement to overlook some highly significant aspects of reality in favor of a reciprocal, private sense of the world. Such an aberration almost invariably leads to trouble; the realities of the world cannot be held back endlessly; the world will take its revenge after slowly impinging upon the bastions of each individual's self-delusion. Here is a situation in which those who have the subtle perception to analyze creatively their position will not, and cannot, do so; in which those who might be of some assistance - Aunt Plantier, Abel Vautier - have not sufficient insight into the characters of those people most seized by anguish.)

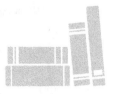

STRAIT IS THE GATE

. . . .

THE SELF-CONSCIOUS NIGHTMARE

The heightened, idealistic, literary prose of their letters dooms the meeting of the young people to be a sad and unsatisfactory charade. So much unreal and reflexive emotion has been poured into the correspondence. Again the question of self-knowledge comes up to puzzle the reader. Alissa seems to make every effort to surround herself with third parties which would lessen the possibilities of any intercourse between herself and Jérôme. On the other hand, she suggests that all their past letters were unreal; that they both had been writing to themselves. So the misunderstandings deepen. It is tempting at first to lay the blame for this almost comical continuity at Alissa's door. But we always remember that Jérôme is quite willing to continue using the rules of the game which they have both claimed for their own. A somewhat new tone does come into Alissa's attitude toward Jérôme, a tone almost of dislike. Something must be going on in Alissa's secret life which we cannot understand. But Jérôme is consistently unable or unwilling to probe further, feeling that such possible probings might alienate Alissa permanently. Such speculations are, by this time, apparently somewhat vain. Because the relationship already seems to hang upon such a slender thread, very little would be required to demonstrate its breakability. Perhaps she represents a pure spirituality, of special devotional commitment which he recognizes in himself, but has not become familiarly concerned with. There is certainly a sense in which both young people project their own narcissistic concerns with themselves on each other. Jérôme's persistent hothouse world, in which he rejects the possible intrusion of the demands and pleasures of the larger world outside, insulates him from aspects of his own self which he is most probably afraid to deal with. He can be seen as using his obstinate, self-deluded courtship as a guard against a larger context of experience; his frenetic insistence on sharing all his inmost thoughts with Alissa merely emphasizes this point, because such insistence relieves him of the burden implicit in self-exploration.

STRAIT IS THE GATE

....

PURITY AND HOLINESS

The word "pure" (or "purity") is used in a number of places in Part VII. An examination of the context of three of these appearances may be helpful to the reader. In one context, we see that the word "pure" is serving as the nominal index of a hope built on an illusory belief of happiness, which only utter self-abnegation on Jérôme's part could bring about. But since Jérôme is not utterly concerned with self-abnegation, since he wants Alissa for his own, the very gesture of kneeling would have served only as a reminder of his impossible and paradoxical situation. The word "pure" is used in our second instance in one of Alissa's letters to Jérôme. She is saying that the ideal love and its greatest possible joy can occur only in the absence of the beloved and in the absence of communication with him. Idealized and "spiritualized" love can hardly go further than this in distancing itself from the physical, social and sensual matrix of living. Jérôme himself uses the word in a third, and later, instance when he describes the impact upon him of Alissa's room. Jérôme starts breaking through the trance-like idealization which has been the characteristic manifestation of his "love" until now. Different as her self-abnegation might appear from Michel's hedonism in *The Immoralist*, we can nevertheless establish one absolutely essential similarity between the two characters. It is not in the specific quality of their actions that we may find such similarities, but in the type of intensity characterizing both. Alissa's behavior in Part VII belongs in the same family as self-flagellation, hair shirts and torturing self-imposed tasks. Her desire to be free from "earthly" bonds is becoming absolute; her disdain for all that partakes of the flesh can no longer be breached. Where Michel found ecstacy in sensual freedom and the flouting of conventional law, she finds ecstacy in utter subjection to the law and in self-mortification. It is interesting to recall that Gide writes in his *Journals* about the self-mortifications to which he subjected himself when a young man in the fervor of his temporary commitment to Protestantism. Both this novel and *The Immoralist* were conceived together by Gide, and were seen by him as correctives of each other, both being the records of deadly excesses.

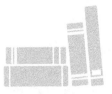

STRAIT IS THE GATE

PART VIII

<hr/>

THE END

The clearly predetermined end of the sad spectacle has now arrived. What saves Part VIII from either mawkish or irritating sentimentality is partly the momentum that has been built up throughout the length of the narrative and the language used. Confronted by such words, used by a man now more experienced in the ways of the world, and angry at his ex-love in addition, what reader could easily shrug off or explain away Alissa's sense of a glory greater than this world has to offer? This terrible and almost unwilling sympathy on the reader's part adds a redeeming power to the pathos of this conclusion. Mixed in with reactions, however, there is another one. It is a sense of immense relief that we have finally passed out of a suffocating hothouse of ever-increasing withdrawal from the world. We never have quite found out what it was in Alissa's perceptions of eternity which gave her such deep spiritual pleasure, transcending not only earthly happiness but life itself. If an attempt is made to compare her life to those of religious mystics, we find ourselves in somewhat of a quandary. For the joy in created things which is so characteristic of, say, St. Francis of Assisi, finds no real counterpart here. Alissa has withdrawn so far from the world that she cannot even praise God's creations for the their beauty, their testimony to God's grandeur. And most likely this is what Gide is trying among other things, to communicate to the reader. Alissa's renunciation and the quality of her "joy" are so bloodless, so self-immolating, that they can rouse in us, at best, a kind of detached, or at times somewhat disgusted, pity for the infinite capacity of man for self-delusion. Ironically the conversation between the two doomed lovers in Part VIII is just about as long as any to be found in other parts of the book.

STRAIT IS THE GATE

. . . .

ALISSA'S JOURNAL

Alissa

In the discussions of preceding sections, we have stated that seeing Alissa through the eyes of Jérôme alone added to the drama, but detracted from our knowledge, our "objective" knowledge. Now, being given this first-person account of Alissa's spiritual life, we ask ourselves how really useful these intimate declarations are. Actually they tell little that is new. What we do learn involves the intensity of Alissa's inner conflict, the force of her desire for life. The ferocity of the inward struggle is appalling, particularly since there is no doubt whatsoever about her profound love. Interestingly she becomes a little more womanly in these final tragic pages. Her journal communicates a terrible, sudden sense of aloneness, a terrifying perception of the atrocious bareness of the walls around her. This is what truly terrifies, the sense that her whole life has been grounded on a baseless series of renunciations and that all the sacrifices have brought her to a death in which she found only further anxieties. It is, horribly, a death which is the absence of the promise for a greater life beyond.

Postscript

The postscript returns to the first person narration of Jérôme, and reveals the tragedy of Alissa's perverse devotionalism. Her own life and the lives of two others have been either destroyed or permanently wounded.

CHARACTER ANALYSES

Jérôme

Jérôme waits, suffers, hopes, is charged with the narration of the story, but is not the main character, if by such we refer to the figure whose activities set in motion the train of events which make up the plot of this "récit." He is, in fact, for all of his involvement, a kind of passive observer. A greater insistence upon action on his part would have made the novel impossible, for it is his delicacy, his worship of Alissa's purity, his respectful observance of her every scruple which prolong the agony in which the main characters find themselves plunged. The love he bears Alissa survives her death, even though in life their contacts were largely based upon illusion and self-laceration. This survival of love ten years after her death leads to questions about the quality of his affections. For in fact his love received almost as little sustenance from Alissa alive as it does from Alissa dead. Why then does he hold to its memory with so tenacious a grip? As we have suggested elsewhere, this dependence upon a wraith, dead or alive, serves to fix Jérôme's attentions onto a figure of the ideal - a fixation removes him from the complex and potentially threatening intrusions of the outer world. It is possible, as a matter of fact, that Jérôme is quite unable to give of himself in love to anyone: we have seen that his concern for Alissa is to such a powerful degree a concern with his own self, however masked. The reader might wonder, with a certain detached curiosity, whether Jérôme is not a potential Michel (see *The Immoralist*). What is it that enables Jérôme to sustain for an apparent eternity such a hopeless commitment? It is either the overweening concern with self which lies at the base of his motivations; or it is the limited amount of raw life energy available to him; or it is the fear of discovering the complex possibilities of life. All these points come into consideration in the course of reading this narrative, since Jérôme's is the central consciousness which communicates with us; and thus an understanding of his character is essential for an understanding of the hidden motivations of both himself and of Alissa.

Alissa

Psychiatric dossiers include cases of "traumatic neuroses," psychological illnesses apparently caused by one extremely severe experience, such as might happen, for instance, in wartime to soldiers. In general, however, case histories do not present such easily simplified patterns. Psychological illness usually stems from a long series of reinforcing difficulties. These speculations bear directly upon Alissa's behavior, even if we choose not to look upon her as a psychiatric case. The incident which contains in germ much of the later narrative detail is of course Alissa's desperate grieving after her mother's faithless running away with a lover. Both she and Jérôme, as children, were judgmentally involved in their sympathetic reactions against this occurrence. These reactions were based on a revulsion, not merely against illicit sex, but against sex as a manifestation of human appetites in general. Their relationship was based upon this understanding. To transcend it would have required the growth of both individuals. We know that Alissa never transcended it. This is a psychological view, but even from the purely moral perspective there seems little doubt that Alissa's sacrifice is presented as waste of life force, delicate, lyrical often, occasionally very touching, but waste nevertheless. She never rises to sainthood. Had the context of the entire tale allowed her to arrive at that level, we would have been faced with quite another story.

Juliette

However tragic Juliette's eventual fate, it has its own grandeur. She occupies a role in the story somewhat analogous to that played by Abel Vautier. Neither could have what they first wanted, but both made choices which, if not the perfect realization of their dreams, nevertheless allowed them to embrace life. For a minor figure she is quite well realized. In terms of structure she is a necessary ingredient in a plot which treats of two people - Jérôme and Alissa - largely unable to communicate frankly to each other. Her activity as go-between, which might have easily become mechanical, takes on a verisimilitude based upon her own emotional involvement in their relationship and her feelings for Jérôme. She is the classical "confidante" of the fictional heroine whom we meet as far back of the classical theater of eighteenth-century France. But she plays a more integral part in the plot structure. The use to which Gide puts her is representative of the sophistication of the novel in this century. We see a similar usage, for instance, in some of the novels of Henry James, in which he presents a ficelle, an artificial means incorporated in a person who nevertheless plays an organic part in the unrolling of the plot movement.

Abel Vautier

As Juliette is the only female character close to Alissa, so Abel plays a role of great importance in relation to Jérôme. As Juliette does, Abel represents the possibilities of a life outside the ethereal and restrictive closures of the book's general atmosphere. Although the bald statement is never made, there is little doubt that Abel's boastfulness, his high spirits, his capacity for **satire** and his humor help Jérôme to retain some degree of perspective in a situation that threatens to engulf him. Both Abel and Juliette are in some sense representatives of the via media, the middle way, which recognizes the challenges implicit in living any kind of life in the world, which allows individuals to effect compromise with temporal duress without sacrificing their entire being.

Uncle Bucolin

Jérôme's uncle sheds a passive sadness over those **episodes** in which he appears. Never reaching the heights of a tragic figure, nor tasting the depths of misery, he lives out a life essentially condemned by the faithless departure of his wife, able at times to find a mild contentment.

Lucile Bucolin

Is her name symbolic? The word bucolique like the English "bucolic" refers to a life influenced by the outdoors, the presence of animals, the freedom to run about, a closeness to nature. Lucile Bucolin is the only individual in the narrative who makes a definitive escape from the closed circle of the little group at Le Havre and Fongueusemare. She represents rife sensuality at odds directly with the respectability and "order" of her surroundings. Hers is the act, as we have seen, which began the entire complex series of thwarted relationships with which the book is concerned. Are we to derive some sort of "morality" from this fact? Should we say, for instance, that unordered sensuality breeds evil and destruction? Or might we suggest, perhaps, that it is the very incapacity of Jérôme and Alissa to share in some of Lucile's traits which dooms them? If any direct philosophical implication is indeed implicit, it probably partakes of both suggestions.

OTHER WORKS

THE COUNTERFEITERS

The Counterfeiters (published in 1927) is his only piece of fiction that Gide recognized as a novel. It represents a departure from his usually serene and simple classical structures to a complex, varied style. Gide wished to structure his novel on the principle of intersecting circles involving several individual destinies. This complexity characterizes the subject matter as well. Gide wanted to mirror all of life, he wished to show all sides of his characters, with their contradictions; if they were not consistent within themselves, reality was to blame.

The novel was meant to be a novel of ideas about the nature of reality. The **themes** of appearance and reality, of apparent versus real motives, hypocrisy versus honesty in human relations are made evident in the subplot concerning a gang of counterfeiters.

The Counterfeiters is undoubtedly Gide's chef chef d'œuvre. The technique of the novel within the novel - its hero is writing "The Counterfeiters" and his logbook of the composition is included - heightens its interest, yet it never becomes an exercise; the characters are pulsatingly alive. The characters proliferate throughout the novel by their connection with the two young students, Bernard and Olivier, and their relationships with the novelist, Édouard. Parents, teachers, lovers, mistresses, friends - all play a part in the lives of the two young **protagonists** and serve to point up Gide's major themes.

The appearance-reality **theme** is skillfully handled in the novel through the actions of the characters. The counterfeit coins are obvious symbols of this **theme**. The myriad possibilities for self-delusion are evident in the presentation of the characters.

Gide wished to stylize his characters, and the irreconcilability of these two propositions - that of mirroring life on the one hand and stylizing it on the other - struck him, or Édouard, the writer-protagonist, as an unsolvable paradox. This dilemma is at the very bottom of the Gidean concept of man.

Gide's ethic of disponibilité, which may be translated as intellectual and emotional availability, is seen as a pattern in *The Counterfeiters*. Gide preached to the younger generation a poetic interest in self-realization and self-transcendence. Mobility as opposed to a static existence, spontaneity as opposed to rigidity of spirit are ethical values to Gide, and are seen embodied in the character of Bernard. Faced with the hypocrisy of his father, Bernard must strike out on his own, he must be his own individual and "become" himself. That he meets constantly with hypocrisy in the guise of people who seem to act honestly is the moral **theme** of *The Counterfeiters*.

Mobility to Gide is important, since to become what we are, we must first detach ourselves from our environments, from the values of society, which can trap us. Bernard says farewell to his family, his environment, in the search for himself, and the search itself, to Gide, contains the fulfillment which is so illusive.

Bernard also displays the Gidean virtue of sincerity. Gide's definition of sincerity is to be yourself, to push aside conventional values to let the real self out. Gide's use of this term is paradoxical, since "sincerity" is one of the most prized virtues of the bourgeois Gide is always warning against. But Gide's sincerity means perfect honesty, not the hypocritical veneer of honesty so often found in conventional men. Such men profess to sincerity, while their motives are far from honest.

It cannot be denied that sincerity, to the extent that Gide practiced it, is indeed a literary merit, inasmuch as the concept of literature as an exploration of human consciousness is certainly a legitimate one. It is here that one of Gide's strong points lies. He saw himself primarily as a liberator.

The chief virtue of the Gidean doctrine is the necessity of being sincere, of avoiding the assumption of a counterfeit personality - this is what the title of *The Counterfeiters* refers to - followed by le déracinement, "uprooting"; that is, the rejection of traditional ties, social conventions, and family influences; la disponibilité, the state of free man who never commits himself; and la ferveur, which is essentially enthusiasm, an impulse towards the embracing of all the joys of life.

Édouard is an excellent example of Gide's ethic of disponibilité. He attacks the family, lamenting the stifling effect on the freedom of the young. Throughout the book, his lack of commitment is evident. And his yearning for mobility is the ending note of the book. Indeed, the book ends as if the action should be assumed to go on indefinitely, in a typically unresolved, Gidean ending.

The Counterfeiters is considered by some to be Gide's greatest work and one of the noteworthy novels of the twentieth century. Other critics find it "strangely defective." Gide himself was defensive of his novel, criticizing his critics for not understanding it and accusing himself of too great a concern for his "art" in the composition of the novel.

The life of Gide that emerges from his books is a superb creative achievement, for without apparently falsifying any major factual information it has produced a mystique, a legend, a cult whose faithful number in the tens of thousands. It should be added that the Gide of the *Journals* is the very opposite of amoral. In vice and virtue he remains a meticulous moralist - or immoralist: the two boil down to the same thing, since both are concerned with right and wrong conduct - who for some reason elicits a note of admiration even from those of us who do not share his views. This may be due to no more than the fact that he was an earnest and deeply tormented man with a basically kindly philosophy.

OTHER WORKS

FRUITS OF THE EARTH

The form of this work cannot easily be defined. The well-known Gide specialist, Justin O'Brien, places the book in the category "Poetry in Verse and Prose." Other critics insist on calling it prose; yet others emphasize the wilfully contradictory elements in the work, and relate them to Gide's penchant toward the confusion of generally recognized genres: we recall in this connection Gide's idiosyncratic invention of the two categories of récit and sotie to take the place of roman, the conventional term which translates to the English word novel. This book has not had significant influence or circulation in the United States, but Albert Guerard points out in his critical work on Gide that few books have similarly influenced two generations of Frenchmen. Germaine Brée considers the book essentially "a spiritual autobiography." It is composed in eight "books," a "hymn as conclusion," and a final "envoi." The writer has not established, nor has he sought to establish, a narrative continuity. This book is a celebration of the immense and endlessly nourishing riches of the earth in all their variety; and the form of the work is as open as the world it worships. Almost anything is allowable; the author's associational fancies dictate what is to be included. The whole is a melange of rhythmed and evocative prose, poems, descriptive lists of foreign places whose names render them more exotic yet, detailed descriptions of what can be perceived through the ears, the eyes, the skin, the nostrils, diary entries, dated and timed, lyrical apostrophes to the imaginary adolescent Nathanael. It is this last formal procedure which gives a continuity to the first three "books" of *Fruits of the Earth*. Here for the first time in his career, Gide talks for himself, and addresses a series of aphorisms and hortatory appeals to the young man....

What is the burden of the message which the "I" of this conglomerate work is attempting so passionately to communicate? Guerard stresses the fact that the word "message" itself may be misleading; so many different readers received varied impressions from the book over such a long stretch of time that we might successfully look at this book as a series of evocations of the natural world on a rudimentary and universal level, a kind of Rorschach test of the spirit. Gide rejects the betrayals of nostalgia, the eroding stages of waiting for insights and fervors; he celebrates the now in its magical immediacy, delights in naming the aspects of the natural world, and takes a new pleasure in the simplest things - which in his state of receptivity strike him with a wonderful strangeness. The author tells of the intense pleasure accompanying his sense of a new birth after spiritual paralysis; he has burned the books, and the idea of the past; he allows the concretions of external reality to possess him - although he does not merge with them. He stresses his desire to be "available," a word of great importance for Gide. By it he attempts to express his opposition to any formulated and fixed orthodoxy which would define a character once and for all; he chants the praises of freedom, freedom from one's family, one's home, attachment, places of rest and refuge, lasting commitments, absolutistic devotions of any sort, freedom from the **conventions** that insist on constant awareness of consequences. Time is now a series of discrete moments, each of which is to be savored for the particular savor it is able to yield. The self must be opened in every possible direction, and it must emphasize the reality of body. Man should be prepared to arrive at the point where he feels no compulsion to choose from among a number of sensual experiences.

We have mentioned the difference of response characteristic of various readers. This difference may also be found in the critical comments of such top-flight Gide specialists as Germaine Brée and Albert Guerard. They disagree about the very architecture of the work. Mme. Brée sees the *Fruits of the Earth* divisible into a 3-1-3-1 sequence. She sees in the first three "books" an emphasis upon the rejection of the past, the sloughing off of dead **convention**, the stress upon living within the needs of any particular organism and not externally imposed "justice." In the fourth "book" however, Mme. Brée perceives a more than slight change of direction. She sees in it a "more critical appraisal." The student will remember Ménalque, the embodiment of freedom and independence who so influenced the young hero of *The Immoralist*; in *Fruits of the Earth* we find another Ménalque, this time named Menalcas, clearly taken again from the type of individual represented for Gide by Oscar Wilde, whose influence upon the writer has been sketched out in the biographical section of this Study Guide. But in this case, Mme. Brée, reading between the lines, perceives Menalcas - who monopolizes this "book" with his philosophical divagations, his reaffirmations of earlier-stated motifs, his biography - as more and more "fatuous, sterile and egoistical." And the following three "books," as Mme. Brée sees them, insist increasingly upon the necessity for the controls proper to civilization, proper to the Christian precepts of self-denial. And the last "book," the eighth, she sees as little more than a travelogue, peripherally connected to the preceding whole. For Guerard, the first seven "books" are characterized by an openness to "light and energy," an openness which he sees throughout offered as ends in themselves; the eighth "book" he sees as an important alteration of this attitude, an alteration by means of which the author is seen as praising a "wise provisional passiveness" which will help him to learn which aspects of what he comes to love are most relevant to himself. The formal distinctions made by these two critics reminds us of the complexity of the author's character and the richness of his matter here. The student will note, in addition, that the work ends with a short "envoi," the first line of which exhorts Nathanael to throw away *Fruits of the Earth* for the sake of his own particular and idiosyncratic growth. Through no one else can the self-earn about its own reality; this very book is only one of the thousand possible life postures.

OTHER WORKS

THE VATICAN SWINDLE (LAFCADIO'S ADVENTURES)

Published some seventeen years after the *Fruits of the Earth*, this sotie could scarcely be more different in tone and structure from that earlier lyrical evocation of passion and freedom. It is interesting to recall that "sotie" is a medieval term, signifying a farce in which the actors mocked the highly placed members of the status quo, often the Church. But this book, although it contains a surface **parody** of the Church - which many, indeed, found irritating - does not so much attack the Church as it does inveigh against the unintelligent lack of awareness typical of most individuals and institutions. Where the earlier book, the *Fruits of the Earth*, manifests an intense, subjective, "sincere" praise for the exfoliations possible within the self, this "sotie" investigates the degree to which men are gullible and short-sighted. It shoots holes in the principles of absolute truth, considers the possibilities of "gratuitous acts," unexplainable by any conventional psychology or theology, and through the fictive manipulation of farcical tone and absurd coincidence creates a complicated form. The book contains five sections, of which the first three bear the names of significant characters as titles. These three sections seem unconnected, but as the reader continues his travel into the book he discovers various connections, familial and other. In the fourth section, entitled "The Millipede," the lives of some of the characters appear to graze others'. The fifth section finds all the characters in Rome for a bang-up finish.

BOOK I: ANTHIME ARMAND-DUBOIS

Two Dimensions, Plus: It is clear from the very beginning that Gide is setting his face against the conventional treatment of psychology and character portrayal common to the realistic novel tradition. His presentation of his **protagonists** is clearly and wilfully "two-dimensional" and farcical. He is not interested in drawing a character "in depth." But a reader with even a relatively small amount of sophistication and a fair amount of attention will not conclude from these facts that the author is failing to "fill out" his characters. It is quite obvious that he is playing another game. And indeed *Lafcadio's Adventures* is a play of ideas, using individuals to embody these ideas. The student, upon reflections, may find it astonishing that the writer whose minute and intense examination of the Michel of *The Immoralist* was based upon his understanding of the complexity of individual mentation, could also be the author of these free-swinging, light-heartedly farcical pages. To a great degree, however, the disparity is more apparent than real, although we will not underestimate the complex variety of Gide the artist. The common link between the two books cited above can be seen to involve Gide's capacity for detachment (a capacity which he did not choose to exercise, incidentally, in *Fruits of the Earth*.) If Anthime and his fellow characters are drawn by a detached authorial seigneur, we must not forget that Michel himself, though a narrator, is skilfully drawn so as to betray himself in the course of his distorted communication. And here we see another common link between *The Immoralist* and *Lafcadio's Adventures*, a link which becomes clearer as the reader gets further into this idiosyncratic work. Almost all of the characters in this book also distort reality, perceiving the world from their particular provincial positions. Such a statement is hardly news of course, but for Gide the relationship between an individual and his environment - particularly his moral environment - was perhaps the supreme interest. A sudden switch in character, in attitude, is always dramatic; that of course is why the Church is presented as overjoyed that a famous atheist and mocker has come into her bosom. But what are the motivations for such a change of position? The forced two-dimensionality of the portrayals does not inquire into such reasons. But the suppression of conjecture in depth does merely increase certain thoughtful tensions for the attentive reader.

BOOK II: JULIUS DE BARAGLIOUL

Lafcadio: Although the Book (II) is nominally devoted to Julius de Baraglioul, the really interesting, and important figure which it introduces is Lafcadio Wluiki - the names of people are themselves a series of euphonious absurdities. Lafcadio, who tells Julius his life story at one point in this section, details the idiosyncratic manner of his growing up. Lafcadio's withdrawal from feeling, from ordinary involvement with other people, is an important aspect of Lafcadio's temperament. He has trained himself not to show emotion, and when he does he punishes himself. He lives on the periphery of established society and finds his brother's conventional work amusing. A conversation between the two brothers discloses the gap between their conception of human character and psychological consistency. It is here that we first meet Lafcadio's - and Gide's - overwhelming interest in the "gratuitous act," which is irreducible to understandable motivation, whether economic, sociological or psychological, an act performed for pure pleasure in its doing, unexplainable by any particular system of thought. This formulation, which throws any kind of causality into question, fascinated Gide's contemporaries, who were attempting the plumb the mysteries of human behavior, but would not accept easy answers, whether Marxist or psychoanalytic. The surrealist movement in art and literature, which emphasized the integrity of the non-rational aspects of human behavior, was interestingly an indirect offshoot of the quality of interest demonstrated here by Gide in the creation of Lafcadio, about he later said that Wluiki was the one character in this book who constantly threatened to become too dimensionally complex.

BOOK III: AMÉDÉE FLEURISSOIRE

Amédée: Fleurissoire is just about the ultimate **parody** of all the quixotic adventurers to be found in so much fiction. The suddenness of his decision to leave on a liberating mission takes the reader completely by surprise. People don't act this way, we want to object, taking off with only the very minimal knowledge of the situation, unarmed by clear information, lacking analytical power, bereft of any reasonable plans. But is not this very absurdity, this cavalier distortion of reality, a significant element in most, if not all, of our actions? Although Lafcadio is clearly the intended "hero" of this book, clever, handsome, now well-to-do, intelligently adventurous, Fleurissoire embodies interestingly the large number of "anti-heroes" which can be found in contemporary fiction. It is in keeping with the ironical tone of the book that it should be poor Amédée who should be passionately moved, in his illusive distortions, to some vague heroic activity. Things really start moving quickly in this section; the standard realistic treatment - analysis, descriptive preparation for scenes, meticulous piling up of naturalistic detail are contemptuously thrown aside by Gide, who relishes the rejection of logical and sentimental causalities. Indeed one section in this Book overtly parodies the realistic techniques of the fictive tradition for which Gide had little sympathy. When Gide recounts the formation of the Blafaphas Fleurissoire Plaster Company he inserts a host of useless details - to the point of adding, in a special footnote, an extract from the catalogue of the company explaining one of its best-selling products. Gide had no care for such plausibilities. In fact he actually inserts himself into the middle of the action time and time again, to comment upon certain activities and personages, disregarding the potential importance of that "willing suspension of disbelief" which so many believe crucial to the success of a work of art. He does not mind "giving the show away," particularly because the show here is moving so quickly, so obviously in violation of the rules of verisimilitude. What Gide wants to do is impress upon the reader the confusion, the complexity, the unawareness, the staggering distortions, the undependability of categories which seem to him to be slighted in the realistic tradition.

BOOK IV: THE MILLIPEDE

Amédée And The Millipede Gang: Poor Amédée, who sees himself as the stalwart champion of orthodoxy, the potential savior of the Pope, becomes inextricably entangled with Protos and his Millipede Gang. This chapter is a first-rate example of Gide's ability to juggle at least two fictive levels at once with utmost dexterity. It would have been easier to create Amédée as a figure of pure absurdity and farce; or it would have been simpler to represent Fleurissoire as a woeful, unhappy victim, imbued with selfless zeal and much to be pitied. Actually Gide has it both ways, a procedure which to some degree explains why the reactions to this book included a heated defense by Catholics of their institution, as well as an appreciation of the book as a Baedeker of social disintegration. The story of Fleurissoire's idiotic misadventures undercuts the traditional picaresque tales of noble energy. The prototypical battles of the great myths are here reduced to mock-heroic absurdities. Fleurissoire's great pitched battles with the insects are prepared for and detailed as if they belonged in the category of historical battles. And, of course, in a sense they do. But the battle is a personal one. It is not hard to sympathize with Fleurissoire's dismay at the insects' approach; we mostly all feel this way. The level of success on this level of reader-empathy is altogether remarkable, particularly in view of Gide's eighteenth-century temperament, which manifests itself in a mode reminiscent of Alexander Pope's reduction of great **epic** activities to the size of minor **episodes** in a lady's boudoir.

Another important element involves the difficulty of ascertaining the truth from any limited position, the myopia of heroes. Luckless Fleurissoire is finally brought so low that he finally ends up as a member - unwitting to be sure - of Protos' Millipedes, the very organization whose chicanery and extortions have set in motion the entire mad affair. In fact Amédée is so completely confused by the end of this section that he sincerely entertains doubt as to what is "real" and what is illusion. Illusion and reality.... Truth and falsehood.... How is anyone to judge veracity, dependability, honesty? These serious concerns of a philosophical nature are set before the reader in a continuous context of unexpected, breathlessly moving narration, one event apparently less likely than another, but what **parody** could possibly capture the excess of real life, of Buchenwald, of Hiroshima? This is a modern book.

BOOK V: LAFCADIO

L'acte Gratuit. (The Gratuitous Action): On a number of occasions, completely by accident and by the action of coincidence, Lafcadio has demonstrated a good-nature and warm-heartedness which prompted him to the performance of generous acts. He has also performed other, minor, generous acts. Lafcadio reasons that these acts were the product of chance encounters and fugitive and random emotions. Why then, if good is the result of chance and needs no ethical justification, should he not commit an "evil" act with just as little ethical warrant - or just as much? It is this general line of thought that leads finally to his wanton and meaningless act on the train. The very method by which Lafcadio decides upon his action is the utilization of pure chance.

Reading the book in the mid-60's adds to it a dimension which could not have been predicted in the second decade of this century. Where it was possible to see in the concern with the "acte gratuit" an interesting literary and philosophical problem or game, later history imbues the idea with more sinister overtones. The history of concentration camps is replete with examples of arbitrary brutality by the S.S., of men chosen at random for either sudden death or crippling operations. The intellectual game of 1914 has become the most urgent problem of the 1960's. Why does a man act in certain ways? Is it possible to analyze his motivations according to a system of thought which is universally dependable? Can we depend upon psychoanalysis for our answers? On Marxism? On sociology?

In addition, this book discloses the author's strong sense of man's infinite capacity for self-delusion. Not only does Fleurissoire fool himself, but even Anthime Armand-Dubois demonstrates the absurdity of his own position, his capacity for self-delusion. By the time the book is finished Anthime has returned to his original intellectual position. And for what reason? Perhaps only because his rheumatism has returned. In any case he stands as an example of the brassy foolishness of any absolute commitment. As atheist he is overly aggressive and grossly unbearable; as believer he is unbelievably humble, saintly to the point of self-immolation and utterly uncaring about what his crass poverty is doing to his wife.

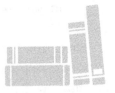

ANDRÉ GIDE

ALBERT GUERARD

One of the important English language critics of Gide, Guerard considers *The Immoralist* the best of Gide's "récits." He considers it an important milestone in the history of the French novel, particularly the French psychological novel, which, he states, was in danger of becoming not much more than a consideration of abstract problems and a **didactic** tool. In Guerard's opinion, *The Immoralist* brought to its category the seriousness and a certain amount of the complexity of some of Dostoevsky's work. He praises the novel for its masterly depiction of the struggle between the conscious and unconscious selves; and he also gives it high marks for its avoidance of certain faults which a more subjective version would have incurred: special pleading, unnecessary "lyricism," self-righteousness. And it is in this connection that he underlines the importance of the formal use of the first-person narrator as the consciousness through which the reader receives the tale. In Guerard's opinion the economy which characterizes the novel is partly responsible for saving the realistic tradition in the French novel. He mentions the fact that most critics of Gide (Guerard writes in 1951) have scanted the novels as aesthetic constructions and have concentrated on the ideas found in them; this attitude is in his opinion unfair to Gide the craftsman. He believes that Michel is a splendid fictional creation, that he cannot be reduced to simplistic Freudian terms. Michel's neurotic experiences, he says, reflect a universal conflict, and *The Immoralist* can, like a great poem, be read and reread. In connection with *Strait Is the Gate* Guerard points out that the contemporary psychological aspect of the book was not an integral part of the novelist's planning: this fact partly explains the divergence between the two portraits of Alissa, the one drawn by Jérôme in which she seems an unnecessarily self-immolating heroine, and the one in the journal which presents a more religious figure. Guerard considers Alissa's journal, or diary, a remarkable document of religious "torment, faith and humility." Without the diary, in this critic's opinion, *Strait Is the Gate* could not have reached the level of success which marks it. However this novel is not as accomplished as *The Immoralist* because it lacks sufficient information to make the texture of the narrative satisfactorily complex and dense. His final judgment of this novel suggests that it was written too slowly over too long a period of time, that it had been allowed to "germinate" too long, and too much was left out of it.

ELAINE MARKS AND RICHARD TEDESCHI

These two critics, who have edited a French edition of *The Immoralist*, also consider the novel the best example of Gide's "récits." They consider that such a work requires at least two readings, the first in order to understand what the narrator is saying, the second in order to read what is behind the lines. Like Michel, the narrative itself, they suggest, is a "palimpsest."

They emphasize the close construction of the book, and accent the fact that nothing in it is extraneous. They also call attention to the close relationship between each of the parts and the narrative rhythm which is typical of each. They point out the achievement of the style. Michel's usual tone in the narrative is flat and grammatically perfect. But particular words rise up out of the otherwise homogeneous context to communicate the sense of Michel's unconscious longings. The critics mention that both Michel and Alissa of *Strait Is the Gate* belong to the same family of "tortured and torturing spirits."

ENID STARKIE

This critic points to the relationship between *The Immoralist* and the lyrical *Fruits of the Earth*, published earlier. Where in the previous book Gide had sung the need for self-realization and the glory of sensual existence, in the novel Gide places these in a moral context in order to study their effect upon people. In connection with *Strait Is the Gate*, Starkie reminds the reader that Gide, in a letter to Paul Claudel the poet, said that his intention in writing the book had been to demonstrate the error of that form of contempt for the world which Alissa manifests. She considers the novel the "most movingly personal" of all Gide's work and praises highly the final scene between Jérôme and Alissa, a scene of great "literary and psychological beauty." She considers that the novel has a harmony of style and a unity of a classical order; the psychology, she thinks, is more sure and deftly handled than before; the minor characters stand up well in their fictional settings. She does remark, however, that the book should have ended with Jérôme's reading of Alissa's journal: she believes that the epilogue detracts from the unity and organic wholeness of the book.

JOSEPH GERARD BRENNAN

In a critical work published in 1964, Brennan underlines Gide's concern with the concept of "sincerity." He suggests that Gide's most abject characters, as well as those most marked by egotism, are the most "sincere." Alissa is "sincere." Brennan points out that it is precisely this attribute which contains the fatal flaw of the characters. Gide is interested in showing that the moral excellence of "sincerity" is a commonly mistaken perception. Many weak and evil men have been perfectly "sincere," lacking a knowledge of the complex motivational patterns which go to create character. Brennan also points out that there is a new emphasis in *The Immoralist*: a utilization of Nietzsche's idea that strength is equivalent to moral right. Although Gide himself denied a significant influence of the German philosopher, Brennan says, there is close analogy between some ideas in the German's *Birth of Tragedy* and Gide's thought. In his book, Nietzsche attributes to the classical Greek civilization tendencies toward both order and chaos. And it is precisely this simultaneity of drives which Gide exploits in his novel. Writing about *Strait Is the Gate*, Brennan sees in Alissa the heroine as Protestant saint. Rather than finding in her final despair (as recorded in her journal) an ultimate sense of alienation and loss, he sees in it the very features of sainthood at its last mortal door. He reminds the reader that Christ himself, in his last words, asked why God had betrayed him. In conjunction with this ultimate model, then, we can estimate the spiritual authenticity of Alissa's journey and arrival.

JEAN-PAUL SARTRE

Sartre, in a general statement on Gide's work, says that the two essential characteristics of the novelist's work include both "courage and prudence." It is the close-lying juxtaposition of these two elements which creates the interior tension of the works. Gide's art, says Sartre, is an attempt to attain an equilibrium between risk and rule. He contains the balance between Protestantism and nonconformism. This antithetical game is what gives Gide his great value. In Sartre's opinion, it is this stance which helped French literature out of the impasse posed by the Symbolist tradition, since that tradition was convinced that only a very few choice subjects were usable as matters to be treated in literature. Gide taught his contemporaries, says Sartre, that any matter could be treated in literature, subject to the rules of stylistic integrity.

GERMAINE BRÉE

Professor Brée stresses that the incipient homosexuality which is to be found in Michel in *The Immoralist* is only one, and at that not even the most powerful or important, force in Michel's personality. All the urges which were latent in Michel, and stifled, come into consideration in the progressive reach for freedom which the novel relates. Both in *The Immoralist* and *Strait Is the Gate*, says Professor Brée, Gide reaches heights of profundity and levels of dramatic intensity which are not found in any of the later fictions.

MARTIN TURNELL

For this critic the relationship between Gide's life and work forms an unbreakable unity. He considers Gide himself a psychopathic case whose "whole nature was bent on destruction and disruption." In the sphere of personal relationships he stresses that Gide's constant purpose was to cause "trouble and misunderstanding." The psychopath, as Turnell defines it, is an individual incapable of either sincerity or integrity; his promises are valueless and merely ploys with which to enchant the gullible. Turnell goes from these biographical speculations to their application to the novels of Gide, and states that in the "récits" can be found the "startling confirmation" of the concept of Gide's essential purposes as destructive and disruptive. He tends to see in Gide a very minor writer of fiction whose artistic universe was severely limited by his personal psychological problems. Gide, according to Turnell, was much more a man of letters than a novelist, an artist. Gide had had one formative experience in his life - his life in early childhood and youth in what Turnell calls "the Protestant cell." Unfortunately Gide wasted his substance in a number of books which diluted the intensity of that experience, rather than putting the kernel into one great book. He "exploited" this experience to make it go as far as he could. This explains, for Turnell, Gide's liking for puzzles, questions and problems and his withdrawal from solutions. Gide's novels are at bottom not much more than "superior examples of the man-of-letters novel."

HENRI PEYRE

Peyre considers *The Immoralist* one of the "few" summits of Gide's career. He quotes another critic, Charles Du Bos, who called the book "the masterpiece of luminous cruelty." In Peyre's eyes, the novel is meant to suggest that freedom is difficult, but even more that freedom is perhaps only real if it is bought with the anguish of other human beings. Ownership after the pride and passion of ownership have passed is itself a great evil. Peyre quotes from William Blake, whose statement Gide later found moving and true, "Sooner murder an infant in its cradle than nurse unacted desires." In referring to *Strait Is the Gate*, Peyre comments that in this book Gide turned his weaknesses to advantages. Gide has no great power to invent incident, was overly concerned with "purity" of structure, cared much more for the inward turnings of personality than for its overt manifestations. Thus in creating Alissa, Jérôme and Juliette, particularly the first two, Gide was able to establish a context which he found temperamentally congenial and formally relevant. This critic suggests that *Strait Is the Gate* is more closely related to nineteenth-century novels than it is to the fiction of the twentieth century: modern fiction is more interested in physiological or psychoanalytical motivations than in spiritual motivations, which are more characteristic of the preceding period.

JUSTIN O'BRIEN

This American critic emphasizes the difficulty implicit in separating Gide's biography from his character. Referring to the possible influence of Nietzsche upon Gide, he comments that Gide is not to be seen as a mere disciple of the German philosopher. One book (Nietzsche's) "is a book of propaganda; the other is a book of warning." When he writes about *Strait Is the Gate*, O'Brien comments that however great the novelist's sympathy is for Alissa, he does not fail to accent the uselessness of her life gestures. O'Brien reminds the reader that Alissa, in her journal, presents the clear possibility that her unquenchable drive toward "holiness" is largely based upon her jealousy of Juliette's happiness when Alissa realizes that her sister's happiness had not really required her sacrifice. Perhaps her "purity" is founded upon a desire to prove "that she is capable" of monumental renunciations.

ANDRÉ GIDE

. . . .

Question: What is the relationship between Gide's life and his work in *Strait Is the Gate* and *The Immoralist*?

Answer: There has been much critical discussion about details in Gide's life which may be traced in these two books; and discussion has also focused upon the finding of material in the books which could relate back to the biography. The relationship between the life and the work is unusually close. Many, if not most, of the incidents which play an important role in these two "récits" can be found in some form in Gide's life. The trip to Africa, the relationship with Marceline, the discovery of Ménalque (Oscar Wilde, largely), the incipient homosexuality, the lure of the young Arab boys - all these incidents in *The Immoralist* may be found in close similarities in the life of the novelist. With Gide, particularly, it is easy to find the similarities because he publicized his private life, both in letters and conversations and also in his *Journals*, autobiographical writings which manifest his desire to find out the truth about himself and to communicate that truth. He even wrote an entire book about his wife, Madeleine, soon after her death. Whatever the dependable truth is in that book, and it is disputed, it serves nevertheless as an instance of Gide's unceasing tendency to publicize his private existence.

Question: To what degree did Gide's religious upbringing play a part in the formation of his thought and his work?

Answer: Gide's Protestant background is essential to what he became. Martin Turnell, for instance, considered it so basic that he entitled his study of Gide's three "récits" *The Protestant Cell*. The novelist's childhood environment predisposed him to the spiritual exercises of which he tells us in various writings. His initial intimacy with Madeleine, whom he was later to marry, had its genesis in the religious and renunciatory impulses shared by both young people. The intensity which informs *The Immoralist* and *Strait Is the Gate* is largely the result of the conflicts imposed on the novelist by his religious and austere childhood and by his directions toward a greater freedom. Only a mind steeped in the particular idiosyncratic movements of Protestant devotionalism could have written Alissa's journal. Only such a mind could have reproduced with such anguishing crystallization both the intense struggle of Michel and the spiritual excesses of Alissa. French literature, which has made an honored place for published correspondences, has benefited from Gide's religious concerns. A long correspondence between him and Paul Claudel the Catholic poet has for quite a while now been a symbolic manifestation of the relationship between Roman Catholicism and the Protestant ethic. Claudel, eager to convert the younger Gide, contributed to a series of letters which can still profitably be read.

Question: What is the quality of Gide's contribution to French literature?

Answer: Opinions on this matter differ widely. We have seen, for instance, that such a critic as Martin Turnell considers Gide, at best, no more than a successful man of letters in a country which seems to specialize in producing individuals to fit into this category. Jean-Paul Sartre, on the other hand, is pleased to see in Gide the revolutionary who brought to the mainstream of French literature the artistic consideration of material long held unsuitable for serious work. Gide has contributed, perhaps even more than any work, or particular works, a stance. It is this stance which appealed greatly to the generation after the First World War in Europe, a generation which felt betrayed by the disastrous outcome of the conflict, by the burial of their most idealistic hopes, a generation which felt quite rootless after the destruction of the old class systems and all the contending ideas and theories - all of which claimed to represent a new hope. To the members of this generation Gide's ethic of disponibilité sounded interesting or, even more, usefully appropriate to their needs. By this word, which may be translated as "availability," Gide indicated the capacity to transcend one's own past, one's own learned patterns. He meant the freedom to operate according to the desire of the deeper parts of one's personality. *The Immoralist*, a critique of the extremes of such a position, nevertheless points out some of its directions. The drive to power which is embodied in Michel, and which negates conventionally Christian ethical attitudes, became an important aspect of the political and ideational spectrum of postwar Europe. Common postwar revulsions against the big-power hypocrisies of great nations in a supposedly Christian West led quite easily to an interest in such Nietzschean ideas. We need look no further than the success of such ideas in the formation of Nazi and other totalitarian states after 1917 to understand this fact. Gide, very much part of his time, and very alert to the intellectual currents around him, exploited a personality which, dealing with its own inner conflicts, produced analogues of a number of the greater conflicts in the outer world.

Question: What generalizations can be made about Gide's writing style?

Answer: Before he wrote *The Immoralist* Gide's work often wandered off into the plush lands of overexuberant lyricisms and the kinds of superficial rhetorical effects which accompanied his narcissistic self-absorption. With the publication of *The Immoralist* Gide's style took on its more characteristic, classical and original tone. This book perhaps includes within its relatively brief confines the most perfect balance of evocative and serviceable prose in any of the novelist's works. Even the other two "récits," good as they are, are composed in a "flatter" prose, in a language which attempts to prune itself of all rhetoric. "Economy," Gide would insist, is the important concern. He was a close student of the history of the French language and used its tenses, its moods, its patterns, its syntax, its vocabulary with a subtlety which repays the closest readings.

BIBLIOGRAPHY

Gide, André, *The Immoralist*, New York: Alfred A. Knopf, 1961 (trans. Dorothy Bussy).

_____, *Strait Is the Gate*, New York: Alfred A. Knopf, 1924 (trans. Dorothy Bussy).

_____, *Fruits of the Earth*, New York: Alfred A. Knopf, 1949. London: Martin Secker and Warburg, 1949.

_____, *The Vatican Swindle*, New York: Alfred A. Knopf, 1925. Or, *Lafcadio's Adventures*, Alfred A. Knopf, 1927. Or *The Vatican Cellars*, London: Cassell and Co., 1952.

_____, *The Counterfeiters*, New York: Alfred A. Knopf, 1927. Or *The Coiners*, London, Cassell and Co.

(These editions are available also in paperback reprints in the Vintage Books series, by Alfred A. Knopf. *The Immoralist* is #K8; *Strait Is the Gate* is #K27.)

Brée, Germaine, and Guiton, Margaret, *An Age of Fiction: The French Novel from Gide to Camus*, New Brunswick: Rutgers University Press, 1957.

Brennan, Joseph Gerard, *Three Philosophical Novelists*, New York: The Macmillan Company; London: Collier-Macmillan Ltd., 1964.

Guerard, Albert, *André Gide*, Cambridge: Harvard University Press, 1951.

Marks, Elaine, and Tedeschi, Richard, "Introduction," in *L'Immoraliste*, New York: The Macmillan Company, 1963.

O'Brien, Justin, *Portrait of André Gide: A Critical Biography*, New York: Alfred A. Knopf, 1953.

Peyre, Henri, *The Contemporary French Novel*, New York: Oxford University Press, 1953.

Starkie, Enid, *André Gide, in Three Studies in Modern French Literature*, New Haven: Yale University Press, 1960.

Turnell, Martin, *The Art of French Fiction*, New York: New Directions, 1959.

CPSIA information can be obtained
at www.ICGtesting.com
Printed in the USA
BVHW071336090321
602012BV00009B/1755

9 781645 420200